Sustainable 5S
How to Use the Lean Starting Tool to Improve Flow, Productivity, and Employee Satisfaction

Published by MudaMasters, Dublin, Ireland
Visit: www.mudamasters.com

First edition

ISBN: 9781096854180

Introduction

Last year, the multinational company I was employed by provided its employees with the opportunity to visit other sites and organizations that were making their own lean journeys. The purpose of these visits was to observe and learn more about the various lean based continuous improvement initiatives that were pursued and to what end. During this fantastic initiative, one German team was inspired to look for the perfect factory environment inside our own company.

According to our headquarters, the best 5S implementation (*the* lean tool for workplace organization) had been done by a factory in the UK some 5 years previously and was still in effect. So, two months later, the management team of the German site flew to the UK for a plant tour. Upon arrival, the German management team discovered however, that the UK factory was just as disorganized as - and maybe even slightly dirtier - than the far newer German factory they had come from.

The first question that arose in everyone's mind was: how could *this* be considered the perfect example of 5S? What they saw in the factory did not at all look like the shiny and well-organized workplaces in the pictures of the slide deck that headquarters had shown them. The only conclusion that could be drawn was that the "standards" which the colleagues from the headquarters had been so enthused over, had not stood the test of time.

Those of you who are already a familiar with 5S, will realize that the UK site had not been able to reach the final stage of 5S: The Sustain stage. In this stage, managers are supposed to take turns visiting the shop floor to make sure the standards that have been put in place are still valid and adhered to. In addition, it's a critical practice within this stage for managers supporting the team in each area to encourage and support them in finding the next improvement to pursue.

In a former role within another company, it had been my job to visit different sites and perform the so-called *maturity assessments*, to assess to what level different lean tools were implemented and utilized find improvements.

During one of these visits to a factory in Sweden, the operators working there told me about their problems in sustaining their 5S standards. The situation was being made more complex by the fact that they were working in a shift system with multiple teams operating in the same working area over a 24-hour period. They had asked for assistance from their manager to support their 5S efforts, but he was too busy with other work and had not demonstrated any interest in supporting his team in their pursuit of a higher-order standard of workplace organization.

In these conditions, I could assume that if I were to come back in a years' time, the 5S program would no longer exist and past improvements would be as invisible as in the factory in the UK that I described earlier.

Lastly, in a third instance, I flew to the US to visit a factory where the 5S system was working perfectly; at least according to the Management team. I went on the shop-floor with the operations manager and site manager and did indeed see most of the 5S tools in place. I saw great standard lay-outs of working areas with shadow boards for tools, lines in the floor that indicated where Work-In-Process (WIP) was allowed to reside to be worked on, and even a posted history of 5S audits that showed that in this factory, management supported the teams in making sure the 5S standards were being sustained; unlike in the other two factories I described above.

So, given what appeared to be a very good representation of the 5S tools, I asked the site manager about the results that 5S had brought him and his team. In other words, I wanted to know what measurable benefit had been achieved with this great implementation? Most interestingly, he had no idea what I was talking about. The teams in the US factory had spent a couple of days in each area to clean and organize each corner of the factory, and team leaders and managers spent time every day and every week discussing these standards with the operators and with each other. But their discussion lacked any consideration of productivity benefits, let alone set targets for the next improvements that could be achieved with 5S.

To summarize my personal experience; I see this kind of inconsistent and incomplete form of 5S implementations in most organizations that I visit. That tells me that the practice of 5S is one of the most underestimated and undervalued lean tools that exist within the entire lean tool box. Even though it is simple in its concept, most teams do not use it to its full potential; namely, improving team productivity, improving the flow of the process, reducing lead times and thereby reducing production costs.

In this book, I aim to help you break that cycle. I will describe how you can make sure your 5S implementation helps you improve productivity from the start, and how to create a continuous cycle of small improvements that improve the experience of your workforce and even your customers. But before we go into details about how to do that, let us start by looking at what 5S exactly is and why it is so commonly used in lean transformations.

Chapter 1:
5S –The starting tool for every lean journey

To begin this chapter, it would be useful to recap some the basics about the practice of 5S. Already in this first chapter, we will see why 5S is and should always be part of all lean initiatives. Spoiler alert: the answer to both questions is that 5S reduces all 8 types of waste.

Secondly, this chapter will teach you the technical detail of 5S. What tools do you need to implement 5S in a sustainable way? You will see that each of the 5S' describe a stage of the program, each beginning with S, and that there are multiple tools available that help facilitate all 5 stages.

1.1. What is 5S

Let us start with the name. 5S is the name derived from the five stages of the workplace organization practice as they originated in Japanese, and sere subsequently translated to English. Each of the five stages starts with the letter S, hence the term "5S". The five words that are most commonly used to describe each stage in English are as follows:

Sort – with the goal to help keep only the necessary items at every workstation.

Straighten (or set) – with the goal to prevent people having search for items and to limit the quantities of items in a certain area.

Sweep (or shine) - with the goal to helps people discover problems at an early stage and prevents dirt from compromising product quality.

Standardize – with the goal to show and documents the agreements at every workplace.

Sustain – with the goal to keep these standards in effect and encourages improvements of the standard over time.

Some companies add a sixth "S", for "Safety" to this list, to make sure safety is taken into consideration when designing a workplace. 5S is then usually turned into 6S, or 5+1S. While I agree that safety should always be taken into consideration when organizing a work place (for instance in terms of ergonomics), I choose to focus this book on the 5S principles and the goals that can be achieved with it in the way that is was originally described in lean literature.

Readers of my book *Lean Transformations* will remember that 5S is one of the tools used at the first level of lean maturity that describes setting the standards in your organization. Only if everybody who works on that workstation agrees on what the safest, most efficient way of working is, can they discuss the next possible improvements.

If these standards are not in place, people may work in different ways, leading to variance in output, lead times, and communication errors because people may unwittingly talk about different problems.

By identifying and demonstrating how a workstation should be organized to work efficiently, and how the work in process is managed, deviations from the standard way of working can and will become visible to the trained observer. This is why 5S is considered a visual management tool. It helps to visualize deviations from the usual state of the workstation.

One good example of a 5S-related organizing technique is the *shadow board*, in which a board is hung on the wall adjacent to the work area. On the board are the tools that are being used by the operator at that workstation in a highly-visible and accessible manner.

The classical implementation of this board involves painting the 'shadows' of the various tools in the location where a specific tool is supposed to be positioned.

When the tool is not on the board, the visible shadow indicates that it is missing. This can help you find or replace the tool before an operator needs it on the job, which can prevent the product from having to wait for the operator to find the tool.

This highlights an important part of 5S. It is not just the organizing of the workplace that brings you the benefits of an uncluttered workplace. It is the culture around using the visual standards that bring you the true efficiency benefits. If a tool on the shadow board is missing and nobody reacts to the visual signal; the missing tool can still lead to a delay in production, no matter how little useless tools can be found around the machine.

5S is therefore not just a technical tool, but a start of a culture in which people think and act in a way based on the visual cues that their workplace organization provides them.

Because of this cultural aspect, it is important for a 5S implementation to be successful that teams define their own 5S standards. This means that as a team is redesigning a specific workstation, they should be discussing whether a certain tool is needed and when to use it, so that they design their own visual cues.

In doing so, they are not only working on the first stage of workplace organization, it is also the preparation for defining Standard Operating Procedures (SOPs) that contain the specific description of how a task is to be performed (which is the second tool described in the first level of Lean Maturity in my book *Lean Transformations*).

Now, before we go into more details on concept and principles in each of the 5S, let's look at some instances in which 5S is applied to organize a space, without us even realizing it, or naming it 5S. I have no doubt that your kitchen contains some 5S standards. You will have a fixed location for everything that you have in there. Pots and pans, cutlery, and glasses—everything is put in the same place every time. Chances are that the things you use most are kept in the place that is easiest for you to access when you need them. For example, coffee cups may be close to the coffee machine, and soap may be next to the sink. Kitchen appliances you need less often might be high up, at the back of cabinets, or even in another room if you don't use them much.

All these "standards" for organizing the kitchen are (unconsciously) helping us to be efficient in the routine tasks that we do in our daily live. When we make a cup of coffee, we never have to look for the coffee cups, because they are always on the same shelf. We don't have to open several different cabinets and wonder where our spouse has put them this time after washing the dishes.

You will also find 5S standards in supermarkets. Fortunately, all vegetables are kept close together, and so are dairy products. Products are also always placed at the same spot every time to prevent you from having to search for them. Imagine what would happen if this were not the case. You would have to search the entire supermarket for all your products every time you went shopping!

The concept of 5S is therefore really nothing new. Almost everyone has been exposed to the concept on a routine basis and even in working environments, I am sure you already have defined some unofficial 5S standards as well to make your work environment more efficient.

The next questions I would like to answer are: what does this workplace organization have to do with lean, and what is in it for any organization that may subscribe to these principles and practices? It is time to get into the *why* of 5S.

Key Point:

- 5S is a workplace organization tool. By using visual management mechanisms, it is designed to make work environments more efficient and effective (I.e. worker friendly)

1.2 Eliminating all 8 Wastes with 5S

There it is: the why. The title already says it all. 5S is a tool that can help you eliminate many types of waste from your process, especially if the people working in the area understand the thinking behind the concept and show the behavior associated with it. If lean is all about removing waste from your process, and 5S is one tool that can help you remove all types of waste that exist, it makes perfect sense to me that all organizations start their lean journey with a 5S implementation.

In the previous chapter we already discussed that 5S is a tool to help you do your work in the safest and most efficient way possible. When I talk about efficiency, I am referring to the speed in which you can perform a given task. The faster a task can be done, the more efficient it becomes. Efficiency can become a competitive advantage when you manage to get a certain amount of output with less amount of effort than your competitors, or in a shorter amount of time than them. But even in general terms, time is a resource that should not be wasted, for it is something that can never be recovered.

This brings us the one of the core elements of the lean philosophy: reducing these different forms of time wasters that do not bring value to our people, our products, or our customer. In popular lean literature, these time-consuming activities are labeled 'wastes', and tradition has it that there are eight forms that these wastes can take on. An easy way to remember them is by having the first letter of each waste category combined together to form the acronym DOWNTIME.

The first waste category is that of **defects**. Whether a broken part, a broken product or a broken machine, all defects lead to delays. And delays will likely result in a decrease in overall operational efficiency.

In a 5S compliant workplace where all parts are straightened and labeled, the changes of an operator from using the wrong parts in production or a wrong tool for the machine can be reduced if not completely eliminated, which means these different kinds of defects can be prevented.

Another efficiency killer comes in the form of making more of something (e.g. parts components, products, inventory) than is necessary based on its known demand. This category of waste is referred to as **overproduction**.

It means you spend material, machine time and/or human hours on (part of a) product that is not yet needed by the customer. Overproduction results into inventories, because everything that is produced while it is not yet needed by the (internal)customer will have to wait somewhere and waiting material is inventory.

In general, most companies keep a little inventory as a buffer for holiday periods in which we do not produce, or for variance in customer demand. These buffers help us to smooth out the variance in demand and can bring stability to production. In purely black and white terms however, it is a waste to spend time and energy on a product if you do not know for sure that the customer will buy it from you and pay you for it.

When it comes to managing inventory, 5S standards will include a clearly defined output area with both a fixed minimum and a maximum number of finished products. A maximum is needed to tell the operators of a workstation to stop producing and therefore prevents overproduction. A minimum is needed to prevent the machine from waiting for material, which is the next category of waste.

The third type of waste is **Waiting**. The link to efficiency is quite simple here: whenever there is a machine waiting for a product, an operator is waiting for a part or an order waiting for a machine or person to be worked on, work is not being done and efficiency goes down.
Reasons for this kind of delay can include a person having to look for a tool, a product or an order. Hence: when the earlier mentioned shadow board includes the tools, a person needs to do his job properly, they never have to search for the tool, and thus the work is not delayed.

The fourth waste is called **Non-used skills** and this waste can be explained in at least two ways: the time people must spend on things that are not directly called for as part of either their expertise or their job description, and the use of people's skills and knowledge to drive improvements and further develop their skills is also considered a waste of potential.
The first type of non-used skills is about spending our time on things that does not challenge them. This type of waste is again about people having to take time to look for tools other than where they are supposed to be.
If I am a trained technical operator, I would like to spend my 7.5 hours per day on engineering my technical product, and not waste one hour per day on looking for the right screwdriver to assemble the parts of the product that I am working on. This type of work also includes the time wasted on mundane tasks that a machine could perform for them.
The second type of non-used skill waste, is not using people's skills and knowledge when we drive improvements. The person who works at the line, knows the line best, and should therefore always

be involved when modifications are planned on that line, to make sure they make life for them easier in practice, not just on paper. Not developing your people to their full potential is second example of this second form of non-used skill waste. Your future generation of leaders might be working in your production line as we speak, so we'd rather have employees spend time on training and improving their skills, than on searching for parts.

The goal of 5S is for people to organize the workplace in such a way that they never have to search for parts, tools, or files, and can therefore focus on what they are really good at; performing the tasks/activities they are skilled in doing and using their expertise to drive improvement.
5S therefore reduces the amount of time wasted on non-used skills.

Transport is the next type of waste and it describes the time that is wasted by moving products around without working on them. The less time needed to move parts and products around, the more time there is available to actually transform them into the product(s) that our customers want to buy.
If 5S principle and practices are not only applied at the workstation level, but to the plant level as well, the standard layout massively influences the amount of transport necessary to move products and parts within workstations and between workstations or departments.

The sixth waste is (excess) **inventory** and in terms of time, inventory typically translates into unnecessary waiting time, because work-in-progress materials and products are stored somewhere waiting to be worked on.
Next to the waiting time aspects, carrying inventory also involves a financial cost as it ties up capital. It represents dead capital since the materials, products or tools are already paid for, but not yet in use.

These materials or products only creating revenue when they are sold to the customer.

The bigger the inventory is, the longer the waiting time of the products within that inventory, and the longer it takes before our paid materials bring the company revenue.

When applying 5S standards to inventory levels, there are typically a fixed number of materials or products that are allowed to be placed in a certain holding area. By assigning not only a fixed location but also a fixed quantity to these products, we can manage inventories using visual cues that we will discuss in chapter 3.3.

Motion is the seventh waste. Where "transport" is the waste in which products or parts move around unnecessarily, motion is waste involving any amount/degree of movement in a machine's mechanisms or of a person's body that is not directly related to creating value for the customer's order. Again, the example of a person walking around looking for a tool, a part or a piece of information is a pertinent.

Within 5S, we focus on the employee reaching for a part, product, or tool with the least physical effort possible, to reduce motion waste.

Finally, there is **Excess Processing,** or "over processing" as this practice is often referred to. This waste includes all extra work that is being done by a person or a machine to get the job done. This sort of "extra" work can take many forms and exists in many places. It typically involves expending more energy and/or effort than is actually required. Rework needed because we created a defect in a product is one example. Spending time and effort in creating a product that is of much higher quality than the customer is willing to pay is another.

By reducing defects, 5S also reduces rework and therefore further reduces any unnecessary expenditure of time and effort.

All of the eight most commonly identified wastes (easily remembered through the DOWNTIME acronym) are addressed through the practice of 5S principles. Accordingly, the full implementation of this practice will result in marked improvements in productivity.

Let us now take a look at what 5S actually is, and how you can implement it in any workplace.

Key Points:

- 5S addresses all 8 types of the most commonly recognized waste... when implemented properly.

1.3 Tools and methods to use in each of the 5S stages

To utilize the 5S model, multiple tools and methods can be used in each of the stages outlined below. The most important thing to pay attention to is the sequence for implementing the 5S model. The proper sequence is **sort; straighten; sweep; standardize**; and **sustain**.

Stage one is referred to as **SORTING**. At this stage, an evaluation of the need for everything that can currently be found in the work area is conducted. For every part, material, or tool in the area, you can ask the question: is this tool/material necessary to perform the task? If yes, the part can stay in the area; if no or if you are in doubt, the part is removed from the area and moved to an open and un-used area of the plant where it can be tagged and displayed; the red tag zone.

The **red tag zone** is a designated location in the factory or department in which all materials and tools can be placed and "tagged" with a read label indicating the item as being "unnecessary" for the operation.
Accordingly, all the items that are removed from different workstations are identified with a red label and moved to the designated area.
Figure one depicts what a Red Tag Zone could look like in practice. Notice that the area is designated by using (red) tape on the floor, and that all items in the area have a label attached to them that is used to document when the item was moved there and for what reason.

Using a red tag zone supports the team in using the 5S principles as a **continual process** rather than a single event. Instead of having one clean out session, parts can be moved to the red tag zone at all times.

In the event that it turns out a part is needed at a certain workstation (either the same one where it came from or another workstation), the part can easily be taken back into the work area and should then be included in the standard (stage four).

Figure 1: An example of a physical Red Tag Zone, and a 5S Red Tag label

One consideration that is important in implementing the red tag zone is the time that an item is allowed to be placed there before it is decided what should happen to it. For instance, if the tool stays in the red tag zone longer than a defined period, it can go back to the warehouse, where it might be able to be reused through hand over to another department. If no other department can reuse the part or tool, it can be thrown away or if there is value in any of the items, it may even be sold or auctioned off to employees.

I've witnessed multiple "5S flea markets" within one of the companies that I have worked for in the past. Tagged items that were tagged out were sold to our employees at very low prices. The profits of these flea markets were donated to charity.

In addition to evaluating if we need everything that can currently be found in the targeted working area, we must also think about what might be needed going forward that is currently not in this area. In other words; while those things that are no longer needed are being removed, things that are needed must be brought in.

Doing the analysis on **what tools should be brought in** to the 5S standards should reduce the chances of operators having to look for tools (motion) and bringing them back to the workplace (transport) times.

Where removing items from a work area (sorting out) can help to declutter the workplace and create order, it is the addition of necessary items to a workplace (sorting in) that has the biggest impact on productivity.

The second stage of 5S is referred to as **STRAIGHTENING** or **SETTING IN ORDER**. After having removed and properly disposed of everything that is not needed by production operations at the workstation, the parts and materials that are needed can be given a fixed location and fixed quantity. Doing so becomes a manifestation of the "**3F**" **principle**, in which every fixed part, has a fixed location, with a fixed quantity.

One example of establishing these standards is the use of colored lines on the floor to show where something is allowed to be placed temporarily.

Note: In my experience, tape is preferable over paint, because of its ease-of-use and removability.

Another example is the use of shadow boards on the walls for tools. The goal of marking the location for each and every tool on the board, is to make it readily obvious when a tool is missing, which in turn should decrease the possibility of productivity decrease because something is missing that is necessary for the operations.

Within seconds (i.e. no more than three), everybody passing by should become aware as to whether something is missing. This is referred to as the **three-second rule**. Figure 2 shows an example of a shadow board from a factory in Italy, where you can see what tools are missing by looking at the shape of the white lines.

Unfortunately, there is no worldwide standard for the use of **different colors** for floor taping. There are however, recommended standards by OSHA and ANSI.

Figure 2: Example Shadow board, where the white lines indicate the shape of the tool is missing

My personal recommendation for use of colors are as follows:
- Yellow: designates the boundaries of the workstation.
- Blue: designates work in process.
- Green: designates finished product.
- Red: designates defects and the red tag zone.

- Yellow-and-black stripes: designates places where nothing should be put—for instance, an area in front of moving doors, machines, or inside walkways.

The third stage is **SWEEPING**, which is an activity that employees would be either partly or completely responsible for, depending on the nature and scale of the workplace.

Each team or individual involved should have his or her own dedicated machines or workstations to clean at routine periodic intervals. Sweeping is therefore an ongoing activity, not a single, one-time event. Having machines cleaned (and possibly even maintained) by operators using them is important because nobody other than the operator is likely to know a machine better than the operator who uses it on a daily basis.

One of the biggest benefits that comes from having operators in the habit of regularly cleaning their assigned machines and/or workstations is that these operators are more likely to **discover small abnormalities** that happen to emerge in use, before they result in producing defects. This means, that the goal of the sweeping stage is not just cleaning the machine, but it sets the stage for the practice of operators responding to deviations from the standard, which is the most important practice within lean thinking and behaving.

Within a manufacturing facility, different work areas can be designated with different colors on a lay-out overview of the facility, to demonstrate which team or individual is responsible for which area.

Cleaning a machine only once does constitute an acceptable 5S standard. Practicing sweeping is about defining a **cleaning schedule** that is most appropriate to making sure that the machines or working areas are always in a proper working order, thereby helping to prevent of avoid possible defects and/or delays.

The same is true for tools on the shadow board. Depending on what industry you are working in, a slightly damaged tool can have a major impact on the quality of your product and on the productivity of your production. It is therefore important to discuss what interval and level of cleaning is necessary in your specific situation.

Carrying out the sweeping stage in any factory can sometimes be a controversial topic, leading to discussions among employees on how best to perform this activity. Keeping the workplace clean is clearly a desirable endeavor and it's an important part of making the 5S model work as intended; particularly when it comes to attaining and sustaining the highest quality levels for the products and/or services being offered to customers.

The time spent on cleaning machines and even floors however, negatively impacts the efficiency of the process on the short term. Spending time cleaning 30 minutes today will cost me 30 minutes of production time today. The challenge will therefore be to design a cleaning schedule that balances the time we invest in cleaning proactively, with the time it saves in the future in terms of less quality issues.
Though cleaning the machine might be related to the technical skills of the employee working there, cleaning the floor is usually not considered a value adding task by the machine operator even though it may still have an impact on your product quality. Who does what part of the cleaning is therefore also a topic of discussion.

Next to the discussion on who does what cleaning and how often, there should also be a focus on reducing the time that is necessary to keep the workplace clean. We will come back to this during the sustain step.

The fourth S in the overall practice of 5S is the **STANDARDIZING** stage. As with every other agreement on the way of working, the layout and organizational agreements of the workplace should be recorded in the standard.

There is an important distinction that needs to be made between something that is *standardized* and something that is a *standard.* The former involves making a practice/procedure something that can be performed in the same or very similar manner anywhere and anytime it is being performed. A good example is when it comes to standardizing all 5S practices throughout a facility. In contrast, a *standard* is something that helps ensure that a specific desired/targeted level of quality and/or performance can be achieved as a result of following the specified standard which often contains specified procedures and/or metrics that must be met.

Also, it's important to realize that both a standardized practice and a standard can be changed over time as necessary. The ability to pursue and make improvements demands that both be changeable whenever a better way or a higher level of performance is desired.

When it comes to specifying a workplace standard for cleanliness and organization, it usually suffices to post a **picture** of the workplace or part of the workplace, along with a sweeping schedule.
It is also good practice to visualize all **3F** (fixed place, fixed part, fixed quantity) information on the floor or walls within the dedicated lines. Again, the main goal of 5S is elevate the ability for any observer to identify abnormalities as soon as possible. For

instance, when a designated location is empty, we would like to know what is missing and why.

Figure 3: Two examples of a 5S standard

The publications of the 5S standards meets that need. Figure 3 shows two pictures of various 5S standards in practice at two of the factories I worked at in the past. The left example has 4 pictures (of different corners) of a working area in its standardized configuration.

Because this standard is posted at the working area, an operator (or anyone) can make the comparison between the current condition of the work area and how it is supposed to be maintained.

In the example on the right, there is only one picture on the document, but it also includes a list of the critical items for that area and a sweeping schedule.

An added benefit that comes from having clearly documented standards, (which in the above examples were one-pagers), is that they can be used as training aids when it comes to training new operators on how the workplace is organized and why it needs to be maintained in that condition.

Finally, the established 5S standards (like all standards) will serve as a starting point for the pursuing the practice continuous improvement. Only when there is a well-documented standard of the current state of the workplace (as agreed upon by all team members), can improvements to the standard be discussed. This is because if there is no standard as a starting point for the discussion, team members might be either improving something that is not supposed to be done in the first place or improving something that was already standardized by others in the past.

Improvements might include the need for fewer tools at a workstation, an improvement of ergonomics, or a reduction of the time needed to keep the workstation clean.

The fifth and final S in the 5S model stands for **SUSTAIN,** and this is the most difficult of the stages to implement in practice. It is difficult because this stage circles back on all the prior stages to ensure that they are being appropriately maintained and updated as necessary. The sustain stage therefore has two main objectives: sustaining the current standard as they were agreed upon by the team and identifying improvements when the standards are no longer relevant or complete.

An aid that can be used to check whether the standards are sustained is a mini-audit. By writing short questions on a **T-card** (a small card in the shape of a T so that it can easily fit a plan board) everyone can perform a mini audit in an area of their choosing. The cards can include questions such as; "Are all materials placed at their specified location?", "is there something missing that you need to do your job properly or better?", "are the tools on the shadow board cleaned according to standard?"

The easiest way to perform such an audit, is by linking each T-card to the standards defined in the previous step, leading to one T-card per standard.

Figure 4 shows an example of a T-card system that is used in a Dutch factory. On the left, a board with different T-cards is shown on which the mini-audit cards are kept and can be accessed on the shop floor.

The right picture shows an example of one T-card in the hand of an operator, on which the use of a team board is assessed.

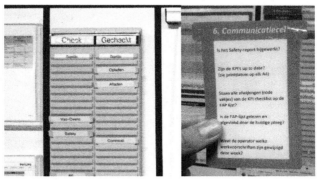

Figure 4: example of a T-card and a mini-audit board

If there is a need for a more thorough 5S audit, it is possible to create a longer **list of questions** using A4 paper. Such a longer list can include different categories of questions.

Firstly, the questions could be listed by groups according to the areas within a department. These corners would represent the locations at a workstation that need to be checked one by one. In this case, instead of 4 pictures on one paper, you would have 4 parts of the audit with questions related to each part specifically.

Secondly, the larger audit form could include questions specifically designed to indicate the level of sophistication on each of the 5 stages of 5S. Doing so would make it possible to assess the 5S maturity of a team, based on their progress on each of the 5 stages. Questions in this kind of audit could include: questions about the red tag zone and its use in the first stage, the use of shadow boards and the lines on the floor in the second stage, or cleaning according to the cleaning schedule in the third stage, etc.

Third, the expanded audit form can contain questions that are designed to measure the overall level of understanding of 5S in the team. Questions such as "what does 5S mean?", "why do we want to implement 5S" and "what advantages does the 5S standard bring you as a team working in this area?" re all useful measures of the extend of comprehension.

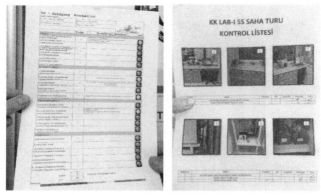

Figure 5: two examples of a 5S audit form

Figure 5 above shows two examples of 5S audit forms. The example on the left depicts an example that I found in Germany which shows the extended format that contains questions for each stage of 5S. The example on the right is a more abbreviated example and depicts a combination of pictures and area-specific questions. I found it in use in a factory in Turkey.

The advantage of having a structured question list is that the answers to the questions can be scored and the overall scores can be tabulated. The **overall score of the 5S audit** can serve as an indicator of the level of maturity of the area and the personnel being audited. You can share these results with the team(s) involved and use it to lay out the next set of action steps that need to be taken to improve the score.

To provide an idea regarding how far it is possible to progress in promoting a 5S initiative, I will share one of the most elaborate **5S board** I have seen thus far in my career. It is shown in figure 6.

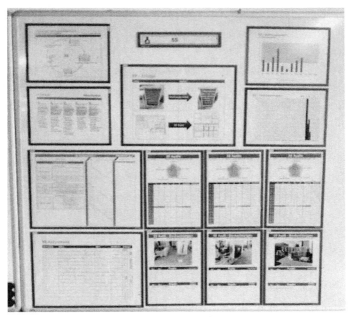

Figure 6: an example of a 5S board

This board includes the following:
1) An introduction to 5S,
2) Before and after pictures of the last improvements of the 5S standards,

3) An overview of who is doing the 5S mini-audits, when they are planned, and when they are done,
4) A list of open 5S actions to improve the standard,
5) The latest 5S score
6) A trendline chart composed of the audit scores over the course of a year for each of the three corners in this area,
7) A KPI record of how many 5S improvements have been implemented on a weekly basis over the course of a year.

When I am doing a 5S audit, and there are no specific cards or forms with questions, I simply use the picture that is displayed as the standard on the shop floor. I compare it with what I see around me. When I see a discrepancy, I can ask a team member what is going on by simply pointing to the standard and asking why the current state no longer resembles the standard that has been agreed to and published.

Based on my experience, I consider the red tag zone (for sorting) and the 5S mini audit (for sustaining) to be the most important tools in the 5S Practice toolbox. They both play a critical role in keeping the 5S model alive and functioning as a key part of daily operations. They help prevent the believe or notion that practicing 5S is just a one-time or a once-in-a-while thing.

For example, when it comes to the red tag zone tool, items that do not belong at a workstation can constantly be tagged and moved to the red tag zone for further action. Anyone is then free to remove it and bring it back to a workstation where it either belongs or is needed. Or—if it turns out that item did have a function in its original area—a fixed location can be created at the workstation and the 5S standard updated.

And that's it! The simple principles of 5S, with its relatively simple tools to implement and sustain each of the 5S stages, and thereby helping to reduce waste and boost both local and overall productivity.

That said, it's also important to keep in mind that "simple", is not the same as "easy". Of all the factories I have visited so far, only a handful of them had a functioning 5S system in place that actually did result in improved productivity levels.

So, that being the case, it begs the question as to what is happening at all the other implementation sites? Why are 5S initiatives not always a success? Answering these questions will be the topic of the next chapter.

Key Points:
- The 3F principle (fixed product, fixed place, and fixed quantity) can help mark locations on the floor and on shadow boards to make it easily evident when something is visibly missing.
- All 5S standards should be documented so that they can be taught to others and used as the starting point for on-going improvement efforts.

- The red tag zone and the 5S mini-audit are two tools that help make 5S a continual process as opposed to simply being a one-time event.

Chapter 2:
Common Problems with 5S

In Chapter one, we discussed what 5S is, and how it can reduce all eight different forms of waste; that is, when implemented correctly. Now to me, this is not rocket science. It even makes perfect sense from the standpoint of being able to get a big return for a minimal investment. Why would any organization not want to implement 5S principles and practices if doing so can help reduce waste and improve productivity, not to mention make the work environment healthier and safer for the employees?

Unfortunately, my personal experience whenever I visit different organizations, is that most 5S initiatives are considered to be failures or, at least, they do not bring about the benefits that are expected or achievable.

In this next chapter, the focus will be on analyzing the situations in the three factories I described in the introduction chapter: one in England, one in Sweden, and one in the United States. The English Factory was the factory in which the 5S standards had completely disappeared after 5 years. The Swedish factory is the one where management did not support the highly motivated operators who were charged with the task of implementing 5S principles and practices, and lastly, the American factory is the one where established standards were being sustained, but nobody really knew the purpose behind doing so. Those workers were functioning a bit like programmable robots, so let's hope it's not contagious.

2.1 5S is Not Sustainable

So, there we were... more specifically, myself and a group of German colleagues were in England at a factory that was supposed to be the shining example of a 5S implementation within our company.

After spending the afternoon on the shop floor observing the current state of the operations, many questions arose. Questions like; "Why didn't the headquarters staff know that interest in and the effort behind 5S had been slowly diminishing over the past 5 years?", "Why did the English site invite us to observe the operations even though their 5S initiative isn't really in place anymore?" and - of course the most crucial question: "why did the English factory Stakeholders not manage to sustain the 5S standards?"

I must say, a root cause analysis on the first two questions would prove very insightful, but for the purposes of this book - which is to help you understand the true power of 5S principles and how to implement it properly so that you can improve productivity and positively surprise your customers - we will only focus on the third question.

Why is it that so many organizations fail to sustain their 5S efforts and end up like the UK plant did? After all, they spend so much time and effort in cleaning and organizing their working areas, but despite this, sometimes within a few months, the newly established standards seem to have been all but forgotten. It seems to me that 5S initiatives that follow this trajectory are a waste of time. Why? Because the time and energy put into it did not accrue any long-term benefits for the company. And that is a shame, because 5S can bring you so much!

In the previous chapter, a number of the various 5S tools contained with the 5S toolbox were covered. If you have read the previous chapter, you may have already guessed what was missing in the UK plant's attempted implementation. That's right, if you want your 5S initiative to have a long-term impact, the following two things are essential: the mini audit, and the red tag zone.

In the short term, the mini audits play a key role in keeping the initiative rolling and on track. Without these semi-official evaluations during which employees check to see if everything is still working as was agreed in the past, it is only a matter of time before the everyday distractions results in an inclination to skip the cleaning of a machine, or make someone forget to return that tool to the board where it belongs, so that it is available for the next shift to use.

One of the most commonly cited reasons for a team's inability to sustain and evolve 5S standards, is that they are sometimes working on a special product that requires a specific tool, a special process different from the normal product mix. The team therefore changes the lay-out for **one specific situation that does not fit the standard**. For me, that could be ok. Especially in environments where you work on hundreds of different products with different dimensions, it might be impossible to define one single lay-out that is useful or appropriate for work on all products.

I therefore understand that in the middle of a shift, tools are going to be in use, and materials might be moved from place to place so that the operator can use them whist working on an order. However, it should be standardized practice, that at the end of the working order (earliest) or at the end of the shift (latest), the workplace is brought back to its clean and ordered standard configuration.

The same way of thinking and behaving apply in the office environment. For example, take a situation where an office worker is engaged in performing a complex digital job for which there is the need to access multiple paper files in order to compile and analyze information. It is not the goal of office-oriented 5S to not allow workers to have huge piles of paperwork on their desk. The goal should be to return the office environment to a clean and well - ordered state-of-being at the end of the day, and only keep paperwork on the desk for the task at hand.

One option for maintaining the necessary focus when it comes to having a clean area at the end of the shift is to display a **leading indicator or a checklist at the team board** (i.e., a display board where the team comes together on a routine basis to discuss performance and possible improvements) and ask the team whether they put all tools, equipment and materials back in their respective standard locations by the end of the shift. This gives the team the opportunity to address the 5S standards on a daily basis, and it helps the team in making sure that no matter how extraordinary the work of that day happened to be, by the end of the working day, everything is back to the standard configuration.

In this example of the individual purpose of the 5S board described in the previous chapter and the daily management structure that uses physical boards to visualize performance, have been combined. The 5S audit results simply becomes one of the performance indicators on the board in this case. And given that these audit results are key point of interest and focus, the team is continually challenged to define improvements that can be pursued in their area so as to improve this 5S score in future audits.

The second tool that makes the 5S initiative a continuous process rather than one clean out session is instituting and utilizing the red tag zone. Having a clearly defined zone on the shop floor that is accessible and safe for people to enter and inspect, preferably in a position where many people pass by, makes it possible to visualize abnormalities and having everybody participate in the process.

Whenever an item is put in the red tag zone -which often occurs after a 5S audit - or whenever somebody finds a part or tool that does not belong in the standard specified configuration, a discussion should take place among the team members that focuses on how a particular item got there and whether or not it is actually needed for the current operation.

This discussion can and typically does lead to taking one of the three possible actions: The first possibility is that the item in question is brought back to its proper standard-specified location. The second possibility is that it is determined that the item is needed in the current operation but is not part of the standard configuration yet. In this case, the 5S standard can be updated to include the new item. The third possibility is that the item is disposed of permanently.

Using the Red tag zone in this way, gives an organization a built-in mechanism for updating 5S standards whenever operational requirements change. In essence, the up-dating and improvements to the standards that is necessary to sustain the initiative is built into the 5S model as an iterative evaluation and improvement loop.

It is important to highlight here that an organization's senior leadership team members have a primary responsibility for making this red tag zone principle work on an ongoing basis. All of you that have read my book *Lean Transformations* will be aware of the fact that one of my favorite quotes is that a tool is just a way of making the problems visible, and that it is the people who must do something to solve that problem. In instances when it seems everyone is ignoring the obvious fact that an item is misplaced and that is now residing in the red tag zone, it will be a matter of time before people stop sorting out the stuff they don't need, and the changes of finding the next improvement of any 5S standard will subside and eventually cease. That is why senior level leadership engagement is vital to any and all 5S implementation initiatives.

That concludes the coverage of the situation encountered in the English factory and brings us to the second factory that I described in the introduction. In contrast to the English factory where the mini audits and red tag zone were missing as key components in the overall 5S implementation so that 5S could be practiced as a continual and sustainable process, the Swedish factory actually had both of these tools in place.

When the tools are in place, but results are not realized, we may have a different kind of problem. This will be the topic of the next chapter.

Key Points:

- Use the mini-audits to maintain the 5S standards
- Use the red tag zone and team discussions to update the 5S standards

2.2. 5S is Not Embedded in the Organization

Lean tools exist to visualize problems, but it is the people who will have to solve them. The true purpose of 5S is to visualize abnormalities in the workplace and to give people the possibility to solve them before they lead to quality problems or delays. In the previous chapter, we discussed the importance of the tagging principle and the audit principle to make sure 5S thinking is embedded in the organization and not just a onetime action.

But what happens if these elements are both in place, but 5S still does not bring measurable results? This was the case in the Swedish factory I described earlier. The implementation team had had a fantastic 5S kick-off training program for their 5S implementation, in which all production teams throughout the factory underwent a full day of 5S training scheduled with an external trainer. The objective of this training was to create the first 5S standards that would be used throughout the initial stages of implementation.

Following this training program, shadow boards were created, machines were cleaned, and there were even some discussions about how to improve the transport of orders between different departments (a topic we will come back to in the next chapter on how 5S will improve productivity).

In addition, the teams posted their first standards on the shop floor using pictures of their respective areas of responsibility. Each of these pictorial standards included a 'view comments' section underneath each picture to explain the most important points for that area. Finally, the team created mini audit T-cards to be completed at least once per day.

Then, after doing all that work and making tremendous early progress, nothing more happened. The teams struggled to keep the standards usable. The reason for their on-going struggle was due to the complexity that was associated with coordinating standards across all the areas involved. Consequently, a few months after the initial 5S training workshops were conducted, every team resorted to creating their own standards and routines, but ignored those of the other teams.

So, the critical question that arises from this case study, is how might this situation have been prevented? Believe it or not, I see these kinds of things happening routinely across a wide range of organizations and operations. It's happening not only with 5S, but also with other programs, tools or processes that are being implemented in an organization in pursuit of operational excellence. Unfortunately, to many of such organizations, the notion of 'deployment' simply comes down to organizing a one-hour training session with all the stakeholder teams, after which the members of these team are left to their own devices to do something meaningful and beneficial with their new knowledge and supposed process improvement capabilities.

To me, the solution to make sure any continuous improvement-oriented initiative becomes part of the DNA of an organization is to make sure it is embedded in the organization's fundamental mode of operating, meaning it should be tightly integrated with all other processes and enabling/supporting tools that are already in place and being utilized on a routine basis.
There are likely at least two other lean tools in use to which the 5S-related principles, practices and enabling tools can tightly integrated: the "daily management structure" and the "leader standard work".

Let's look closer at each of these existing lean tools beginning with **the daily management structure**. This structure involves the conduct of daily stand-up meetings in which the performance targets that have been cascaded from the top of the organization to the shop-floor (often via process of policy deployment or, in Japanese, Hoshin Kanri). These performance targets are posted on team boards and reviewed daily. Any problems that exist related to these performance targets that cannot be addressed immediately at that level are escalated back up from the shop-floor to the top of the organization so that the senior-level managers can perform their function in support of each of their teams in any on-going problem-solving that needs to occur. This back and forth series of feedback loops is graphically depicted in figure 7.

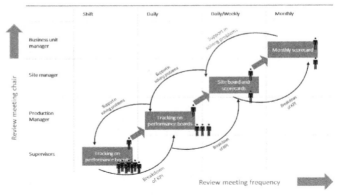

Figure 7: Daily meeting structure example

The intention behind the daily management structure is for every team to have a 10-minute daily meeting (typically held first thing in the morning at shift change), during which yesterday's performance, as well as today's goals are discussed among the team members. Each team has targets that have been created specifically for their department, but they are directly linked to the targets of the overall organization. For instance: a production team has a target "time-to-complete" one order or production batch (usually specified at the shift level), which is directly related to the weekly production plan that has been targeted (typically at the production system level), which in turn influences the performance indicator that is being used by the site management team to measure on-time delivery performance for the entire site (for instance... On-Time-In-Full performance, or OTIF for short).

What makes these meetings especially interesting is when visual management methods/tools/techniques are used to its fullest extent possible. What an observer likely sees is that the agenda of the meeting is represented by the physical board itself, on which different targets are made readily visible through the consistent use of colors and graphs. Many times, green is used to indicate when a KPI is on target, and red is used when it is not on target. To improve productivity in the particular work area being depicted in this example, actions will need to be defined and followed-up for any red KPI. All such actions and follow-ups are also posted on the board and made highly visible. Figure 8 shows one example of such a team board.

The daily management structure is just one of the many powerful lean tools available and for any interested readers of this book, it is described in far greater detail in my previous book *Lean Transformations*. For now, in the context of a 5S implementation, I would like to focus on how the daily management structure can be used to support the on-going/sustainable practice of 5S principles.

Since all team meetings are typically conducted in front of the team board - every day using red and green indicators to discuss performance - the topic of on-going 5S performance and any related actions/interventions can be readily added to the board.

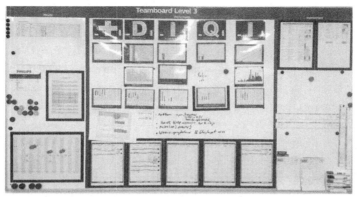

Figure 8: example team board with on the middle part;
KPI's, trends and Actions

When it comes to posting KPI performance on a team board, each indicator should be clearly identifiable and include a graphic representation of its trend over time, meaning that it's readily observable as to how the team's performance relative to each indicator is changing over time; preferably in the direction of a desired/ targeted condition or end state. If the trend line is static or flat over time and/or not changing in a desirable manner, actions that have been defined by the team may not have been sufficient to solve a particular problem and bring about a desired change. Accordingly, the need for a more dramatic intervention can be escalated to one level higher in the organization.

As depicted in the picture of the team board in figure 8, the board contains all the elements described above. Specifically, in the middle part there can be seen five red/green indicators that the team members can use to color code the current days' performance in either red or green (typically one month's performance is displayed per piece of paper). Below that, a plot of the performance trend throughout the year to date of that same indicator is being displayed, and on the bottom of the board, all the actions that have been determined necessary for the on-going improvement of each specific indicator can be seen.

Clearly using this sort of daily management structure lends itself well to addressing 5S-related issues as well. Teams can discuss their own actions, problems and even publish the results of their 5S mini audits on the team board (either next to, or instead of on a separate 5S board). In the event they are not able to break through having mere discussions and are not able to engage in the actions needed to sustain and improve the standards that have been established, they will have no choice but to escalate the 5S-related issues to the next higher-level team meeting. Of course, it will then be up to the management personnel above the team to respond in a proper way; that is, in a way which is supportive of their teams and provides them with the resources they need to solve the problem(s) at their level.

When the practice of 5S is linked to the daily management structure, all layers of the organization are then participant in the 5S initiative, meaning that when people have issues at the shop floor level, they should be receiving support from their manager(s), or the manager(s) of that manager, to help resolve whatever issues cannot be resolved directly on the shop/production floor.

The second tool that is often practiced by organizations making the lean journey and should be linked to the 5S initiative is referred to as Leader Standard Work. This tool defines all the standard work that needs to be performed on an on-going basis by the indirect (i.e., non-production) functions and all management personnel. Leader Standard work specifies all tasks that each function needs to accomplish and calls for the use of a tracking form similar to one used by the shop floor teams, again using red/green colored performance indicators on a daily basis.

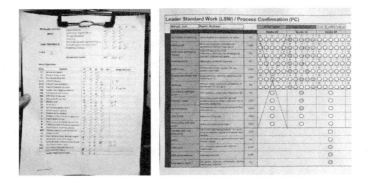

Figure 9: Leader standard work examples

Above in figure 9 are two examples of a leader standard work template. You can see that there are actions that need to be done routinely on a daily basis (with a white box that is to be ticked every day), a weekly basis, and a monthly basis.

When employing this lean method/tool/technique, there are two keys to its successful implementation. The first, involves having 5S mini audits discussed in every leader's standard work. Now, of course, it's possible to simply list the task "5S mini audit in Area X" as a weekly to-do on every leader's agenda, but wouldn't it be even more effective – not to mention being a manifestation of higher-order thinking and behaving - to also describe the need for making some improvement to one or more 5S standards as part of it?

That being the case, if a change to each leader's task description were to read: "Perform 5S audits and find one improvement", it would be much clearer relative to what the real goal underlying the conduct of these audits happens to be; specifically, finding the next 5S improvement in pursuit of improved overall performance of the system or Enterprise.

Unfortunately, simply stating a goal going out onto the shop-floor and engaging workers in 5S discussions is not always enough to bring about the desired change in the prevailing pattern of thinking and behaving. Fortunately, there's more that can be done to help reinforce the need for and motivate the desired change. This is where the color coding of the leader standard work comes in. Because the template is set up as a KPI, it's possible to use the template to track the success rate on the daily management boards in each work area as well.

Using this approach to defining leader standard work and building into the activity the need to make on-going improvements means that there will always be a regular discussion centered on whether every manager in the organization has finished all the tasks on their daily and weekly lists, and if not: what might need to be done so as to make sure the audit will be completed as required/expected next time?

From my own personal perspective, I am not so tough that I would want to see a score of a 100% completion rate. I know that corporate life can be challenging and demanding, and that there are always going to be some important issues that can distract one from doing what needs to be done and consume the time needed. As a consequence, it may not be possible to go to the shop floor to do a 5S audit on any particular day. However, in a 4-week period (the way the leader standard work template is set up in figure 9 above) it would be difficult to imagine that one would have no time at all to conduct the mini audits. Accordingly, based on my personal experience, I would strive for a 3 out of 4 success rate in this example and have a discussion with the team of managers if it came down to them never finding the time they need to be able to conduct these audits.

The good news about having these sorts of conversations with team leaders is the fact that they may lead to the creation of other improvement possibilities as well. Time pressure is only one possible reason for somebody not going to the shop-floor to complete the mini-audit. It could be possible – depending on how the 5S program was introduced and how new hires are being oriented that an individual does not realize how important 5S is to sustaining productivity in his/her work area or throughout the entire production operations. Or, maybe there's someone who just doesn't realize how important 5S is their manager or team leader.

Linking 5S to the daily meeting structure and to leader standard work are just two ways to help you embed 5S in your organization and prevent it from being a stand-alone process or project. Accordingly, it should lead to workplace organization problems being addressed at the appropriate management level and help everybody in the organization improve their 5S standards so that the layout of every workplace can be as efficient and effective as possible.

Key Points:

- Link 5S to the daily management board to make it part of the daily discussion in the organization.
- Make 5S part of leader standard work to have every leader involved in the 5S discussions

2.3 5S Does Not Improve Productivity

Now let us imagine, for just a minute that you have implemented everything I wrote about in the previous chapters. You have implemented the 5S standards in every workplace, the entire workforce is trained to keep them up to date with mini-audits, the results of the audits are published on the daily management boards, and even managers are doing their rounds and ticking off their actions on their Leader Standard Work checklist. There are only two questions that would need to be asked and answered under such circumstances: 1) Why are we doing this? And 2) What is the benefit of having people doing all these small audits every single day?

These questions would help the American factory I described in the introduction. The system worked like a well-oiled machine in which every person played their part on a "basic" level. More specifically, everyone walked their mini-audit rounds, but despite that fact, doing so did not help the team to further improve performance. That being the case, we need to dig a little deeper to understand why.

If you have read the previous chapters on the goals of 5S, you may have already figured out the answer. If the goal of 5S is to improve productivity by reducing the eight types of waste, then it's also essential to make sure that the same three tools discussed in the previous chapters to support and encourage continuous improvement are being utilized and in evidence: the mini audit, leader standard work and the team boards. Let us now look into detail how there three tools can help you to get more focus on productivity improvement, starting with the mini-audits.

The **mini audit** is traditionally used for 'sustaining' the fifth "S" of 5S, but to me, sustaining is only half of what it can do for an organization. If stakeholders within an organization know that the mini audit can be used to define improvements in the workplace, the questions that will be incorporated into the audit will likely be different than when the audit is not being used in this manner.

I therefore recommend a two-part 5S mini audit structure for pursuing continuous improvement. The first part consists of special use questions related to sustaining the current standards, and the second part includes questions that help define the next improvement that needs to be pursued.

In the first part, the following are examples of the types of questions that typically appear in a mini audit:
- "Does each tool have a fixed location on the shadow board?"
- "Is the cleaning schedule being followed?"
- "Are the orders worked on in the proper sequence?"
- "Can anyone/everyone see within 3 seconds if the production plan is on schedule or not?"

In the second part, the following are examples of questions that explore improvements in a work area that could be asked of the person responsible for that station:
- "What would you like to improve in this area?"
- "What is the biggest waste in this area?"
- "Are you missing any tool or information allow you to perform your job in a way that's better?"
- "What is your biggest frustration at work?"

The goal of these questions is to start a discussion about how further improvement(s) to the 5S standards could be achieved. Not surprisingly, these sorts of discussions also demand the ability to develop and engage a different skillset by the people who do the mini-audits. That skill set involves a different way of thinking and behaving, and it begins with a change in attitude from simply checking on current conditions, to more of a coaching/mentoring orientation. With this new way of thinking and behaving it becomes possible for those individuals who are conducting the audits to coach colleagues and help them discover possible future improvements in the work environment and even in their own abilities to identify and solve problems.

The second tool that can be used to establish a greater focus on productivity improvement is **leader standard work**. Again, the proper use of this tool is dependent upon the language that's used in defining the task of the manager. When a manager's task is defined as "do a 5S audit", the implicit expectation is something less compared with when the task is defined as "find a 5S improvement with an operator in area X". It is all about managing expectations and adjusting wording to reflect a new way of thinking and behaving.

As part of my leader standard work, I would block out 1 hour for my *gemba walk*: the lean term for going on a walk in the factory to talk to people, learn about the processes and discuss improvements with the people who do that work.
My goal in conducting these gemba walks was to find at least 1 improvement that could be made in the factory. Sometimes, all that was necessary for me to realize this goal was to visit one area and have one conversation with a colleague. But on most other days, I had to visit up to 7 different areas and have 7 short conversations, before I came across one improvement while working together with an operator. On some other days, the audits would not result in any improvement at all, which for me is totally fine.

I believe it to be unreasonable to expect every manager to find an improvement every single day. However, if this trend continues over an extended period of time and a manager is unable to find any improvement opportunities whatsoever, something is wrong, and the manager is likely in need of some coaching that will help him or her conduct their 5S audits in a more productive manner.

The third tool that can be used to help team members better manage their work areas, are the **team boards**. When used as part of the daily management system, they can help to guide the discussions of all teams in discussing the eight wastes and how best to go about minimizing or eliminating them completely. In this regard, readers of my book *Lean Transformations* already know that I am a fan of having five categories of measurements on each board: **safety, quality, delivery, cost,** and **people** to help focus attention on critical operational issues/concerns. In this regard, I suggest that teams use the cost column to measure the type of waste that is most common in their work area so that they can address it on a daily basis.

This means the teams should already have a clear idea about the biggest waste(s) in their area. If they do not have any idea, conducting a *waste walk* would be helpful in developing and maintaining this perspective. Accordingly, the *waste walk* is one of the tools described in the next chapter.

Changing the conversations that occur during a 5S audit and during team meetings is a great starting point to creating and sustaining the sorts of productivity improvements that are typically desired and expected from a 5S implementation. But the best way to implement 5S would be to have these improvement discussions with the team as you start your first 5S workshop.

The next chapter will describe some additional tools that can be utilized when a 5S initiative has not yet been initiated. In essence, these are tools that can help prepare the way for a 5S initiative so that there is a greater likelihood that the first 5S implementation attempt is a measurable success.

Key Points:

- Include questions that encourage improvement in the 5S audits
- Include "finding an improvement" as a task in leader standard work instead of "do a 5S Audit".

Chapter 3:
Preventing these problems in your 5S implementation

In the previous chapter, I highlighted what went wrong in the factories in Germany, Sweden and the United States with regard to their respective attempts at implementing 5S. It was in that context that I revealed the countermeasures that were brought to bear on the problems that existed in these example situations.

In the previous chapter, I described one organization (the English factor) that had not successfully implemented 5S on their first attempt. Their issue was to be able to sustain it over the longer term. Should this be the case for your organization, it's more than likely that the teams involved have not implemented the red tag zone and the 5S audits properly.

In addition, I described the Swedish factory, where the practice of 5S has been successfully implemented and was being sustained at some level, but it was not leading to real change in the way of continuous improvement. In this case, the practice was not connected to other improvement-related processes and practices in the organization such as the daily management system and leader standard work.

Finally, as described by the example of the American factory, if there haven't been any measurable improvement(s) in overall productivity coming about as a result of on-going 5S activities, it's probably because a waste analysis has not been performed and/or the right questions are not being asked in the 5S audits and/or Leader standard work.

These are all relatively simple concepts (though simple is not the same as easy) that can be readily applied as fixes even after having figured out that there is one or more of these problems in the organization.

This chapter will focus on how to maximize the advantages of 5S, even though an organization has not yet started its full deployment. The keys to making this possible involve: 1) deciding where in the organization it would be best to conduct a 5S pilot so as to maximize the chances of realizing the desired results from that pilot, 2) teaching/presenting 5S as a continuous process rather than merely as a clean-up session, and 3) make sure "action management" is in place, so that results will become measurable in the shortest amount of time possible.

3.1. How to pick a 5S pilot location

The first step toward pursuing the fullest realization of the maximum potential benefit from a 5S deployment is to choose the best location to initiate a 5S pilot. There are many possible ways to identify this location. However, the best place to begin and most crucial, is identifying teams that are ready, willing, and able to participate. Next, the location within the factory needs to be taken into consideration. Accessibility, ease of moving things around, potential impact on overall production or the complexity of the area in which the pilot could be conducted are all important factors. Also, if it's especially important to get measurable results as quickly as possible, the 5S pilot would ideally be conducted in the area of the production operations that is currently limiting the performance of the overall process; in other words, in a bottleneck area.

Bottlenecks are typically easy to recognize. They tend to be the slowest process step in the production stream and, as a result, tend to have a recognizably large amount of inventory that is building up in front of it. The reason for the inventory build-up is simple: it's because that step or work area cannot keep up with the established flow through the rest of the production line. The result of these bottlenecks is typically the idling of the process steps and machines that come afterwards. Therefore, to maintain the desired flow, it's vital that the productivity in this bottleneck area be increased. Whenever a bottleneck has been successfully resolved, there is typically a direct impact on the productivity performance of the entire process and the positive effect will be noticeable in multiple departments.

Very often, one of the quickest and easiest methods for identifying and documenting a bottleneck or problem area in the end-to-end production process is a well-known lean tool that's most often referred to as: **VALUE STREAM MAPPING**. This tool is designed to provide a visual or graphic representation of the entire flow of materials and information through an end-to-end production process. It also allows for documenting the amount of time a product or service spends in a process on a step-by-step basis. From the beginning of the process to end of the process, the total amount of time required to complete an order is the "lead time", or "production lead time." Most importantly, the Value Stream Map (VSM) is capable of depicting exactly where value is being added to your product or service (process boxes), and how the product flows (either efficiently or inefficiently) through the entire production process; not unlike visualizing a stream of water flowing over some terrain.

A Value Stream Map (VSM) is typically made up in 6 elements, which are drawn using a step-by-step approach. One example of a Value Stream Map is shown in figure 10. Here are the steps that were followed to create the map:

1. Draw the process steps – where the products/services are being worked on and value is being added as they progress from step to step.
2. Draw the data boxes – these boxes contain relevant information of interest about each of the steps such as: process times, cycle times, downtime, change over times, or Overall Equipment Effectiveness.
3. Draw the interconnection mechanisms being employed between the process steps – these show the way that inventory is being managed between the steps, and there are multiple options here.

4. Draw the linkages that exist with both customers and suppliers – is the product being made to stock or made to order?
5. Create the lead time ladder with all processing and waiting times – this is where it becomes clear how long it takes to create one order for a customer, as depicted both inside each of the process steps and as waiting time between the process steps.
6. Draw the information flow – this is where the information needed by each of the process steps is displayed such that each step knows what needs to be work on.

These six steps are labeled in figure 10 below; which shows a relatively simple example of a paint production process consisting of three steps: pre-batching, mixing and filling paint.

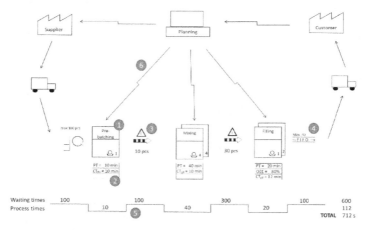

Figure 10: Value Stream Map (VSM) example

If you've never seen a VSM before, this picture probably looks complex. That's because there are a wide variety of different symbols that are used to depict all the elements that typically are found in a production process such as the process boxes and the connections between the process boxes. For a much more complete overview of the most used symbols in VSM, have a look at **www.mudamasters.com** and search for "VSM template".

As mentioned earlier in this section, it's important to be able to identify those process steps where there are actual and/or potential bottlenecks that can interfere with the overall process flow. And this is where it's possible to make use of Value Stream Maps to determine the step or steps that are limiting the speed of the entire line so that a 5S pilot might be conducted there. The part of the VSM that can help accomplish that is step number 2: the data boxes.

Depending on the particular issues the VSM is being used to address, the data boxes can be used to display various time-based metrics. Usually, the choice between **different measures of time** is based on developing a complete picture of the performance of each workstation such as: takt time, cycle time and process time - all of which will be described in more detail below. These metrics are just three of the most commonly used measures. And of the three, cycle time can be further divided into different kinds such as: maximum allowable cycle time, designed cycle time and effective cycle time. Let's look at how these different measures of time are either calculated or measured.

Figure 11 below depicts a breakdown of these different times. Quite often, it's important to be able to make the distinction between them when analyzing and improving the flow of a particular value stream. I'll discuss the horizontal lines in the diagram first, and then the times in the stock diagram.

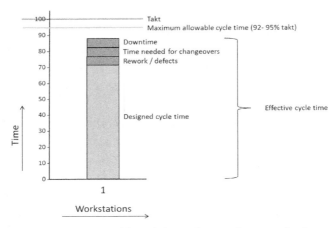

Figure 11: A visual breakdown from takt to cycle times

Beginning with the **TAKT TIME**, this is the interval over which customer demand for the product that's been accruing over some time period must be balanced/aligned with what needs to come off the production line each shift. It essentially becomes the heartbeat of the factory; and is a calculated time based on the available production time for a period (i.e., a shift) and the number of products that are in demand over that same period of time:

> *Takt = [Available Production Time] /*
> *[Customer demand for product X]*

For example, looking at a typical workday in a factory, the available time in Western Europe is seven and a half hours or 450 minutes (i.e., from the standard eight-hour shift, subtract thirty minutes for a paid lunch break, and the available production time is seven and a half hours).

If there is a customer demand for fifteen units per day, the production line takt time would be seven and a half hours or 450 minutes divided by fifteen units, which calculates to thirty minutes per unit. This means that there should be one good-quality finished product coming off the line every thirty minutes if the pace of production is to be able to fulfill the customer demand.

Looking back at Figure 11, the takt time is the top horizontal line. And if the sum of all other times (making up the stack) stay below that line, then the customer demand can be fulfilled.

When it comes to designing or redesigning a value stream, it makes most sense to design it in a way that the takt time is NOT met exactly. Rather it is more common and indeed sensible to build in small time buffers in plant's daily operating schedule that can be used to compensate for small, periodic interruptions that occur to the normal/desired process flow and represent the potential for variations in cycle time.

Building in this time buffer allows for a periodic anomaly to occur, or maybe something could occur that forces an operator leave his or her workstation for a few minutes. These small interruptions can and do occur (ideally only on a very limited basis) and should never lead to a late delivery, which is why building a small-time buffer into the overall end-to-end process or value stream is often the right thing to do. In essence, this is achieved by establishing a cycle time that is below the targeted takt time.

CYCLE TIME is the average measured time required by at least two products to make their way through the process and, as stated earlier, there are three kinds that need to be distinguished from one another: **maximum allowable cycle time**, the **designed cycle time**, and the **effective cycle time**. These are the times that can later be compared to the takt time in order to determine if the process is capable of delivering the customer demand. Here's how that works:

The **maximum allowable cycle time** describes the maximum cycle time that the company's manufacturing engineers should design into the end-to-end processes in order to make sure the needed/desired customer demand can be met within the desired/targeted time period.

For instance, if the needed takt time is 100 seconds in order to meet the current level of customer demand, it's good practice to plan for a production capacity that allows for a production rate of one product every 95 seconds. This allows for a 5 second buffer just in case something does go wrong; and in all likelihood, eventually it will.

How big to make this time buffer depends on the cycle time of your product. Usually, a good rule of thumb is to establish the maximum allowable cycle time between 90 and 95% of the target takt time. Taking this approach is depicted visually in figure 11 with the use of a second horizontal line.

The **designed cycle time** is the calculated time it will take for a workstation to produce a product when there are no interruptions. This is what the engineers plan on for the line when it comes to the theoretical performance potential of a machine and the entire production line. When the engineer(s) of the machine are from an external supplier, they actually have no idea what customer demand might look like for a particular company, and what a target takt time might be. Accordingly, a machine's theoretical/potential designed cycle time, could be completely different from the internal takt time that's calculated for meeting customer demand. Secondly, the actual operating speed of any particular machine could be technology and/or process dependent. As such, it's not always possible to simply increase the speed of a process so that it matches customer demand.

The third type of cycle time is the **effective cycle time**—or actual cycle time. This is the measured time between two or more products or units of output that meet or exceed the established quality specifications. It represents the actual rate of production - produced in practice - or, in other words, the designed cycle time plus any interruption(s) that occurred.

Note: These interruptions are actual measured time intervals and can include: machine downtime, delays because of changeovers, and also the 5S-related wastes (like waiting time due to searching for material or tools, and rework due to defects). These sorts of process interruptions can be categorized in any way(s) that make the most sense. In the example depicted by figure 11, they are shown as the darker-gray stacks.

Whenever effective cycle time is being discussed, a person can measure the time between two good-quality products at the end of a workstation so that, when drawing a value stream map that documents effective cycle time, multiple intervals should be measured in order to get a reliable and truly representative measurement.

Where cycle times describe the interval in which products come off the line, **PROCESS TIME** is the time a product spends within a process step being worked on. Process time can be measured using the so-called "red-dot principle."

Here's how that works. Begin by marking a random product with a red dot and measure the time from the moment where the part moves into a machine or workstation until the moment it comes out on the other side without any machine stoppages. When dealing with a manual workstation and there is only one operator on one workstation and that person is working on only one product at a time, the process time equals the cycle time.

All these times are necessary to analyze the flow of product through a Value Stream and identify possible improvement opportunities. But when it comes to determining where best to start a 5S pilot; it's where the effective cycle times (i.e., the actual measured interval between two good-quality products that we can compare to the takt time) are the longest. It's in these locations with the longest effective cycle time that the overall speed or throughput of the Value Stream is being determined and can be improved.

Note: This is not the same identifying the process which has the longest process time. If a product takes 40 minutes to complete a pass through a process-step (i.e., the process time), but work can be done on 4 products in parallel because the process contains 4 machines operating simultaneously, that group of machines can be said to deliver one product every 10 minutes on average (the cycle time).

Looking back at the VSM example in figure 2, it can be seen that the three workstations have an effective cycle time of 10, 10 and 12 minutes respectively. If the productivity or throughput of the 3rd workstation, the filling line, were to be improved by reducing its effective cycle time from 12 to 11 minutes, the entire output of the process would be improved. Also, it would be reasonable to assume that the basis for making the improvement is the fact that there was customer demand for more of the product.

By evening out (aka synchronizing) the effective cycle times in the different process steps, the end result is often an improvement in **the "flow" of the process**. *Flow* is another widely-used word within the lean lexicon and it implies that products should always be moving or *flowing* from one end of a process to the other. If a does not continually flow or move, it is in a "waiting" state, and *waiting* is one of the eight wastes. The fact that different effective cycle times do exist in a process hinders its maximum potential flow rate because orders or units end up having to wait their turn at those locations with the longest effective cycle times. These end up being process bottlenecks.

In the paint example depicted in figure 10, notice that individual cans of paint are being pre-batched and mixed at a rate that's faster than the rate at which they are being filled. This means they have to wait for the filling station to be able to be filled. In theory, that means that the pre-batching station and mixing station end up experiencing intervals of downtime while waiting before they can start working on the next batch. If they continued processing cans of paint without stopping the inventory levels would stack up in front of the filling station (i.e., the bottleneck step) and would likely end up going through the roof.

So, what would most likely be the impact of a 5S pilot in the filling area? If the result of that pilot were to be the removal of waste from that process step, productivity there would increase, thereby resulting in a reduced effective cycle time; which means the difference between the production rates of the three workstations would become smaller; thereby improving the flow or throughput of the entire process!

The next chapter will focus on the means to do exactly that: make sure that the first 5S pilot undertaken results in improved productivity.

Key Points:

- Use Value Stream Mapping to map the process in terms of its various cycle times.
- Then, by using 5S in the area with the longest effective cycle time first, improvement can be made in the flow of the entire process.

3.2 How to make sure your first 5S standards improve productivity

Now that the process step which determines the speed of the entire, end-to-end process has been determined (using the Value Stream Mapping tool), it is time to dive a bit deeper into the details of what's actually happen in that step. In so doing, it will be possible to see how its productivity can be improved using 5S. There are two tools that can be of help here: the first is referred to as a process map and the second, as mentioned earlier, is the waste walk. As this chapter progresses, it will become evident that these two tools are complimentary to one another can be utilized hand-in-hand.

A **PROCESS MAP** is a detailed graphic depiction of all the steps that are being performed within a specific workstation. It is like a flow chart in which every small step the product or service goes through within that area is graphically annotated. And because this tool provides important information to anyone reading it, it's possible to into as much detail as might be necessary to establish a clear understanding of what's actually happening, and the level of detail captured depends on the nature of the goal that needs to be pursued.

For instance, when a transition is being made from the Value Stream Mapping level as depicted in Figure 10 into the details of the processing steps being performed at the filling workstation (because that is the process step with the longest effective cycle time), it's important to begin the process mapping endeavor by observing each of the **process steps** in more detail and then, label them based on what's being done: prepare the can, fill the can, and move the can to the pallet. I could however also go into a more granular level of detail by dividing up the preparation-of-the-can step into multiple smaller steps: pick the can, put a label on the can, move the can to the filling line, etc.

The goal is to get to the level of detail that's needed in order to identify the eight types of waste discussed in chapter 1.2. In so doing, it becomes much easier to see how the 5S principles can be utilized to identify and reduce any waste that exists, and thereby improve productivity.

Over the years that I've been leveraging the process mapping tool, I have learned that there are many ways to visualize the process map. More often than not, it is a flow chart like picture that employs different symbols for different types of sub-steps. Because I like to combine the process mapping with an analysis of time and make notes about the wastes I see, I use the format shown in Figure 12 which is a tabular format.

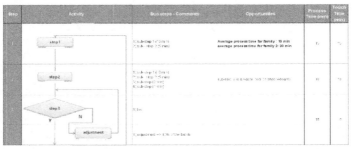

Figure 12: Example set-up process map with Waste analysis

In the activity column, the main steps of the process are listed in the sequence in which they are performed, first at the top and last at the bottom. I also make it a point to graphically distinguish working/activity steps from decision-making steps. As such, more icons can be utilized to whatever extent is deemed necessary or appropriate. The traditional process mapping approach makes use of 6 symbols, with symbols for Process Steps, Waiting, Delay, Transport, Measurement, and a symbol for a Decision.

I display the Measurement and the Decision steps in the way it is usually shown in traditional flowcharts; that is, with a diamond. Based on the result of the Measurement, there are typically two ways that process step can be continued (e.g., go/stop, do this/do that, continue/repeat, etc).

In the sub-step column, I write the details of the activity including a small break down of timings as well. For instance, in step 2, there are four sub steps, and they take about 10, 6, 2, and 1 minute respectively. Detailing this step helps to break down each activity in smaller tasks, where it becomes possible to identify one or more of the eights wastes. In the filling station example, I would write 'preparing the can' as one step in the activity column, and 'pick the can', 'put a label on the can' and 'move the can to the filling line' as three more-detailed sub-steps in the sub-step column.

Whenever I observe a waste, I write it in the opportunities column. That being said, it is important to realize that these observations are to be made within a certain time frame and serve as a snap shot of the current situation. And until the person making the recordings becomes very familiar with the operations, it could be that the waste that was observed and recorded is not a usual condition. Accordingly, it's a good practice to always have the person making the observations and recordings discuss their observations with the person/operator that was observed (or his/her entire team) to find out whether or not what was observed is, in fact, a long-term structural problem or a one-time occurrence.

In the final two columns, I document the total process time for each step and the time that a product or component is actually being worked on by the operator or machine. First, the process time for each step is the time that the product spends passing through a particular step. And finally, the touch time the actual amount of time an operator spends working with that product or component. Performing these measurements can also help in the identification of waste(s). Here too, as was the case when working at the Value Stream level, if the process time for any particular sub-step is longer than the touch time, the operator must either wait (a waste) for a sub-step to finish or must go and do other work in the meantime. Under these conditions, it's likely that other work may be waiting until the operator becomes available to do it.

Once all the sub-step activities in a process step have been identified, it's possible to sum up the different times in the space located below the second to last column. This summation number then represents the total process time for all of the process activities being performed in the higher-level box of the Value Stream Map. And when combined together, all of the sub-step process times should be equal to the total process time for the entire Value Stream. It's then possible to calculate the effective cycle time based on the number of machines, people and the available time for each of the production steps that are depicted at the Value Stream level.

Now that insight into how to go about tracking observations has been gained, it's possible to explore the details associated with performing the **WASTE WALK**.

When constructing both the Value Stream and Process Maps, the best way to analyze the production steps and sub-step activities/tasks respectively is via **direct observation on the production floor**. Since all wastes are considered to be non-value adding activities, they are typically not mentioned as part of a production step or activity description when they are discussed in a meeting room. Therefore, the first good practice tip to follow whenever engaging in mapping endeavors is: go to the shop-floor (often referred to as the "gemba"), the place where the actual work is being done, to learn first-hand about the current process.

A second highly-effective practice associated with any mapping endeavor is for the persons doing the mapping to learn how to do perform each of the process steps. The operator(s) who perform the activities on a routine basis can then teach the people doing the mapping how to perform each of the activities. Then, as a result of learning how each activity is performed, the persons doing the mapping is likely to have the extra motivation needed to ask the right questions to really understand the what, why, and how of each step and/or sub-step. I realize that, in some cases, when an activity is complex or when there are legal requirements, it is difficult and unrealistic to have someone unfamiliar with work performing certain activities. In those cases, it's best to stick with the practice of observing from a distance.

A third good practice tip in making observations is to observe different people doing the same task, and/or different products that are being worked on in the same area. This not only provides more data for the time analysis, it can also can reveal that there are different ways of performing the various activities (some of which are likely to be better than the others) which will also help in the on-going search for improvement opportunities. Whenever there are different ways of doing something, only one way can be the safest and most efficient way of doing it. Finding this way and standardizing it a critical practice when it comes to engaging in continuous and sustainable improvement.

A fourth good-practice tip in identifying waste(s) involves making use of a form which lists all eight wastes in a table (see Figure 13 below). To use this form, a person would need to observe a production line for 30 minutes (or longer) until they have identified at least one example of each of the wastes. This is what one of the lean forefathers of the Toyota Production System (TPS), Taiichi Ohno, used to ask his managers to do and it is what later became referred to as the "standing in the chalk circle" exercise.

Ohno would take a manager out onto the production floor and draw a circle with a piece of chalk and instruct the manager to stand in the circle (which was drawn on a location that the observer would not be interfering with the processes). Then Ohno would tell the manager that he was not allowed to leave until he had found the crucial information needed to resolve a specific problem. The only thing Ohno allowed his managers to do while in the circle was observe. Today, this same practice is widely used throughout Toyota and other companies that are engaged in the practice of on-going continuous improvement.

When using the table shown below in figure 13, write down the work elements (i.e., task/activity) that are being observed; breaking down the entire process into as many work elements as is deemed appropriate (just like in process mapping).

For each of the elements being documented, write down the duration of the element, and make note of any waste(s) that happen to be observed during the performance of that work element. Do so by putting an "X" in the column that corresponds to the specific waste that was observed. In addition to recording an "X" mark, it's also good practice to write down the time that was wasted in the same column.

Waste Walk - Observation Sheet											
Department /Area:		Observer name:								Date:	
Step No.	Work Element	Value Adding	Observed waste (and duration)								Improvements opportunities
		Duration	D	O	W	N	T	I	M	E	
D = defects	O = over-production	W = waiting	N = Non-used Talent		T = transportation		I = inventory		M = motion		E = excess-processing

Figure 13: Waste Walk Template example

The biggest single constraint facing any organization is time. It's essentially a universal issue that – more often than not - needs to be addressed in order to improve and make progress. Based on my personal experience, I can guarantee, that most people who have spent any time working in an organization could identify multiple examples of waste and even come up with multiple suggestions as to how to go about making improvements to the process(es) they are familiar with to reduce and ideally eliminate the amount of waste that is present. All that is required to tap into this latent knowledge is to give members of the workforce enough time to do a proper waste walk and document their observations in any area.

In summary, if it's seen as being important to make sure that the first 5S efforts attempted result directly in improved performance, then it's vital to make sure the pilot is identified based on the results of a Value Stream Mapping effort, and that the waste observations clearly identify and quantify the issues that need to be addressed before defining any 5S standards. In this regard, it's also vital to provide participating team members with the time they need to make the needed observations, and to create the process maps that will help all stakeholders improve productivity.

3.3 5S is a visual management tool which helps to prevent problems

5S is much more than just a way to keep a desk or work area clean. It is a tool to boost productivity (as described in the previous chapters); but there is even more to it than just optimizing standard work routines.

As discussed in the previous chapters, when 5S is properly implemented, it should be possible to see a problem in any particular area within a matter of seconds. This makes 5S a very powerful aid to the practice of visual management. When implemented correctly, any deviation from the established 5S standards can be readily identified and immediately lead to corrective action before an undesirable situation results in bigger delays and/or problems. As such, an effective implementation of 5S helps to buy time when it comes to solving problems. An effective 5S implementation not only helps in defining and establishing standard work routines, but it can also aid in establishing non-standard work routines, as in potential adaptive response to problem situations.

One example of preventing big delays using 5S involved the use of a shadow board which was located next to a machine in one of the factories in the Netherlands where I used to work. It was a glass tube factory, where in one of the processes melted glass literally drips out of a big furnace. As it drips down, it cools into a glass tube in a continuous flow. New quartz-sand is continuously added to the furnace, so maintaining a continuous flow of glass on the bottom end was crucial to the process.

Sometimes, when the sand would not have been properly melted, the hole in the bottom of the furnace would clog. If unnoticed and uncorrected, the situation would result in major problems.

Accordingly, the operator would only have a certain number of minutes before the entire downstream line would shut be down, and the furnace itself would be at risk of overflowing; thereby leading to a whole set of other problems that were both significant safety concerns and very costly.

Fortunately, when the glass and not-fully-melted sand mix clogged the furnace, it could be easily pulled out using a special tool; a long metal pole with a hook on the end. Whenever there was a clog in the furnace, an alarm would go off on a terminal board to alert the operator and he or she could quickly grab the tool and unclog the furnace.

To be able to do that though, it was important that this tool is hanging close to the furnace at all times. It made little sense to run the risk of an operator having to go and search for the tool whenever the furnace was clogged. This example shows the importance of the visual management aspect of an effective 5S implementation. Any and all tools critical to performing an operation are to have a fixed location next to every machine or workstation, but there also needs to be an obvious visual mechanism that is capable of alerting operators when the tool is not there. That way, it's possible to for anyone to notice that a critical tool is missing before a piece of equipment, such as the furnace in the example just cited above actually malfunctions.

This is where the principle and practice of utilizing **shadow boards** comes in handy. It is one of the most widely used ways of visualizing a 5S standard. The shadow board, as the name implies, is a board which depicts shadows of the tools in the exact spot each tool is supposed to be located on a particular board.

As a result of utilizing these shadow boards, when a tool is missing, it's possible for anyone looking at the board to see a potential problem because the shadow of the missing tool is now exposed. And because the shadow represents the profile dimensions of the tool, it's possible to identify the exact tool which missing. And if the shadows portrayed in a bright color, like red, it's even easier to spot the missing tool not only during dedicated 5S mini audits, but just any time anyone is passing by the machine/workstation and its associated shadow board.

A second example of using 5S as a visual management aid is the standards that are being used to visualize **incoming material** for a particular workstation. Again, the goal here is to visualize a problem before it becomes a costly one. Hence, being able to see that something is missing before a machine or workstation has to go into idle mode while waiting for it is a major waste avoider. In this regard, a more detailed look at the 3F principle from chapter one is worth reviewing; that is, having a fixed product, on a fixed location, with a fixed quantity.

Using the same glass factory in the Netherlands that I described earlier, there were several cardboard boxes of standard dimensions that were used to send the finished glass tubes to the customer. Each box would have a standard location in the room. All boxes were sorted from small to big along that wall, and a picture of the box with its dimensions were posted on the wall above each type of box to show which box could be found where (i.e., the fixed/specified product, and fixed/specified location).

The number of boxes of each particular type that were needed each shift varied. Because there were multiple lines producing multiple products in order batches of many different sizes, the local team had to find a solution to make sure that the needed boxes would not run out. What they came up with was quite innovative: they painted the wall behind each stack of boxes in red and green at various height levels, thereby visualizing whether any particular type of box needed to be replenished or not. When the wall behind a stack of a particular type of box was red, it was a visual signal to the warehouse team to deliver new ones. Whenever it was green, there was enough material to keep the line running for at least another 4 hours.

The colors on the wall represented a visual signal to everybody passing by as to whether or not there was enough of a particular type of box. Having this sort of visual signally mechanism in place also improved the productivity of both the warehouse and the production operations, because production did not have to actively order new boxes or make a special request for whatever was needed. The visual management system worked on its own and no replenishment forms or action was necessary from either functional area; thereby representing savings in money, time, and resources.

Another example of the use of a color coded visual management mechanism can be seen in Figure 14 below. In this example, there is room for 12 barrels in total, and the red, amber, and green squares painted on the floor are all of the same size (from right to left). As the barrels are consumed, the colors on the floor are revealed. So, when the red square is reached it's time to replenish the supply of barrels.

Note, however, that it could be possible that another product being stored next to this one has a different split of the 12. If a product is being used at a rate that is greater than the rate visualized in this figure, the red square could be sized so as to cover the footprint of 6 out of the 12 needed barrels, or possibly even 8 out of the 12. The purpose of the color coding is to send a signal for replenishment at a particular point in time. And the bigger the 'red buffer', the more time a logistics/supply department would have to replenish the supply.

Figure 12: Red-Amber-Green inventory levels on the shop floor

If a product is being used at a rate that is greater than the rate visualized in this figure, the red square could be sized so as to cover the footprint of 6 out of the 12 needed barrels, or possibly even 8 out of the 12. The purpose of the color coding is to send a signal for replenishment at a particular point in time. And the bigger the 'red buffer', the more time a logistics/supply department would have to replenish the supply.

In addition to this example, there are other examples of organizing the incoming and outgoing material in such a way that less management attention is needed. In the book *Lean Transformations*, I describe all different kinds of pull mechanisms that automatically pull material from a preceding workstation, without the need for any extra interaction between or involvement of operators and/or managers (hence: another productivity improvement opportunity).

The most important aspect of any visual management tools/mechanism is that anyone can see when there is either too much, or too little material waiting in front of a workstation: meaning that a machine might be idling soon. Supermarket like storage and First-In-First-Out systems are designed for exactly that purpose: they help manage inventory to both a minimum and maximum levels in a way that allows replenishment to automatically take place before the material is gone completely and avoid overstocking.

When done well, all pull systems work on their own, which is why they play such a big role in Lean Management. Using 5S methods to visualize where inventories are supposed to be, and how much material is allowed to be waiting in a certain spot, helps to identify problems before they escalate into unwanted and/or undesirable delays in the production flow (e.g. waiting machines).
However, these pull systems only work when everybody in the factory responds to the visual signals that they provide. Accordingly, **management behavior**, as indicated throughout this book, becomes the key to successfully implementing and sustaining these mechanisms and systems.

If any manager passes a workstation where a tool is missing on the shadow board, or a location in the factory where incoming material is low, and he/she ignores it, that manager is indirectly letting his/her colleagues know that it is okay to ignore these visual clues.

Maybe on the first 3-4 occasions when signals are ignored, nothing will happen. But shortly thereafter, a machine or workstation might run out of supply inventory because of the simple fact that there was no working mechanism to replenish the supply. What a horrible way to let an operation's productivity go down the drain.

One final tip concerning the material replenishment system is to add questions related to it to the 5S mini-audit card or sheet, to make sure the person who does this audit does not only look at tools and the cleanliness of machines, but also at the flow of material.

Key Points:

- Use 5S standards to create visual aids when something is missing
- Train your workforce to respond to these signals.
- Set the right example as a manager and respond to these signals.
- Add questions about the material flow to the 5S audit card or sheet

Chapter 4:
Surprise your workforce and your customers

I hope that it has become clear from the preceding chapters that 5S is so much more than a simple cleaning exercise. It is one of the most valuable tools that you can use to introduce and sustain stability in production operations and help to continuously improve productivity. In addition to this variety of technical benefits, there are also soft benefits which may be harder to measure/quantify, but nevertheless are invaluable. This can include; improved employee satisfaction, reduced pressure on managers, and finally - and most importantly, an enhanced customer experience.

4.1 Less stress and increased employee satisfaction with Proper 5S

First and foremost, when considering what the experience of an organization's workforce might be, a good **5S implementation will bring stability to the processes that they work in**. Imagine how nice it would be to know with certainty that the workforce will start their day with a list of orders to work on, and then be able to work exactly according to that plan without interruptions because no tool, part, or piece of information required has gone missing?

I've found it to be quite surprising exactly how many organizations I have visited do not have this kind of stability in their processes. The members of workforce in too many organizations experience daily routines that are filled with interruptions and extra work most often because a certain material or tool is missing. Under those conditions, a manager may have no choice other than to change the sequence of production so as to be able to continue to make use of the available capacity on the line. Naturally, doing so could lead to all the people working around the line having to drop whatever they are doing and prepare to begin work for another order; maybe even involving major changeovers on machines, and extra parts needing to be ordered from storage.

These kinds of unexpected and undesirable interruptions could then lead to the breaking of even more of the standardized practices that are designed to help maintain a stable performing system. For instance, whenever there is a First-In-First-Out pull system in use in which orders are worked on in the exact same sequence as they are prepared or released into production, and there is a missing material for one order, the sequence might be changed to keep the machines and people working. When this happens, it could lead to having other prepared orders that are already being worked on at other workstations having to be moved around as well. This sort of things can become rather confusing after a while, thereby increasing the likelihood of making mistakes and creating more waste.

In the worst-case scenario, all other workstations must follow the first change, meaning that there is the possibly that all people involved in the process are going to have their work affected because of that one problem on that one machine with only that one order.

Now, as I generally view this sort of undesirable situation, it would be very stressful to work in an environment like that, and I know from my many conversations on various shop floors, a lot of process operators feel exactly the same way. Instead of using valuable capacity and resources in reworking and re-planning the process steps, there's no question that it could be better spent on understanding why a part or some needed tool(s) were missing in the first place and doing something to prevent that from happening in the future.

One of my favorite topics to discuss with operators is the shift-based production system, where teams must work either morning, afternoon or night shifts, and discussing how they must make the switch between them when their turn comes about (there are many different systems to choose from).

The surprising part of these conversations to me is that most of the people indicate that their favorite shift to work is the night shift. They actual prefer to work at night, even though it interrupts their normal biological rhythm of eating and sleeping. And do you know why that happens to be the case? It's because during the night shift, there are no managers or indirect functions, like Quality, Engineering or other technical departments, that are inclined to continuously change the plan. On the night shift, the workforce can simply produce according to an established plan. They have a more predictable experience at work.

I for one would like to see this kind of orderly operation be available for the other two shifts as well. I would prefer to see everybody being able to feel that they can come to work and have a clear sense of purpose relative to what needs to be worked on that shift and, at the end of it, to feel they can readily confirm that they have done everything they were supposed to do to maximize their value added contribution. That means all interruptions should be prevented, and that the best way to do that is to either avoid them or capture and correct them when they are still small. Ergo, using 5S principles and practices such as the visual cues that indicate when something is or is about to go missing is a major step toward achieving this higher-order state of being.

To understand what an organization's or team's current-state starting point happens to be, I like to take note of the number of interruptions that are recorded **on the daily management board** in situations like this. And as a reinforcing indicator, I also like to ask the question as to whether or not the team members had everything they needed (tools and or information) on a particular shift to do a proper job and realize the production plan. When the answer comes be as yes from everyone, the indicator is green, and when the answer is a no, the indicator is red.

So, in every instance where the indicator is red, it's an indication that there might be an opportunity to pursue a 5S improvement. Such an opportunity could take the form of ensuring that the necessary visual cues are in place, or that the minimum quantity of material is sufficient to cope with typical interruptions. Or maybe there's an opportunity to add a new tool to the shadow board. The discussions centering around these opportunities should lead to further improvements of the 5S standards and, over the longer-term, reduce or eliminate the instances where people were missing needed information, material or tools.

When these issues are appropriately resolved/addressed, one by one, it becomes evident in the number of times a tool or piece of information is missing. the frequency either goes down or goes away completely; thereby indicating that it has become easier for the members of the workforce in general and the teams in particular to get on with performing their daily job routines in accord with standard practices. Under these conditions, work also becomes more fun, or at least people get less annoyed, because nobody likes it when things are missing or inventory runs out 'for the one hundredth time this week.'

As a team leader, or a manager that happens to be attending one of these daily meetings, he/she should listen carefully to the discussions that the team members are having; especially when it pertains to something that was missing for the tenth time. This sort of dialogue is indicative of a huge opportunity here, both in terms of improving employee satisfaction as well as productivity.

Having a comprehensive and consistent 5S system in place for incoming materials greatly facilitates smooth, uninterrupted material flow throughout the factory and should prevent the plant management team from having to reprioritize production. Such a system should provide the visual means to identify any missing parts before an order is started so that it doesn't have to be interrupted at the point when an operator make the discovery in the middle of the production operation.

Such a system allows an operator to continue working according to plan, with little to no unwanted stress, and crucially, no unwanted and avoidable annoyance.

Next to the missing information/material/tools issue, **a clean workplace** also leads to the creation and maintenance of a happier place to work. I cannot imagine what it is like to work in a place where you are afraid to touch the machine or cart because it is too dirty and there's no good way to tell what operating condition it happens to be in. So apart from what the dirt might do to a product's quality, or machine uptime, its presence also directly impacts employee satisfaction even though not many people enjoy the cleaning process itself.

This is why the best 5S implementations not only focus on keeping every workplace clean, but also on how best to make it easier to keep it clean over the longer term. As a way to achieve this focus, it's worthwhile taking measurements of how much time it takes for the team to clean up their workplace at the end of their shift (which should also be part of the measurements done in the process map described in chapter 3); and then conduct a waste walk to determine where the difficult aspects of the cleaning process happen to be. With that information in hand, it's possible to define and pursue improvement opportunities that will reduce the time it takes to keep the workplace clean and make the overall process much easier for everyone involved.

When it comes to making the clean-up process easier and more efficient, I have seen amazing creativity in this area; ranging from technical modifications to big machines made in a UK facility that help to lift the entire machine so that it is easier to sweep the floor underneath it, to putting fabric 'socks' on piping to prevent a spillage from immediately forming a puddle on the floor in a Swedish production operation. Any small stain in the sock fabric served as an indication that there is a leakage; and it did so long before there was any potential for somebody slipping as a result of the accumulation of a full puddle.

Key Points:

- Stability of the process is one major factor in employee satisfaction, so preventing missing tools or information from contributing to process instability is achieved by updating the 5S standards.
- Measure the number of times a tool, material, or information goes missing as an indicator of potential problems on the team board.

- A clean workplace is a happy workplace, so keep coming up with improved ways to keep all of the working areas clean as part of your 5S standards.

4.2 Proper 5S = Less problems for managers to solve

When 5S is implemented properly, it's not unusual that the way managers spend their time will undergo a dramatic shift. Within a relatively short period of time, they will find themselves spending their time on solving more complex problems, working on projects, or engage in work activities that are of a more strategic nature, rather than running around the factory floor looking for the missing items needed to keep production flowing.

Over the past decade, I have visited and worked in many factories, and I found that the vast majority of which seem to be **stuck in firefighting** mode. Not only were the operators spending too much of their time running around continuously looking for parts, tools and new orders to keep their part of the production line running, but the managers were stuck trying to keep the lines running by applying quick fixes any way they could. These, to me, are signs and symptoms of operations that either do not have a 5S program in effect or where any existing 5S implementation is not embedded in the organization to its fullest extent.

When 5S principles and practices are being utilized as described in the previous chapters; that is, as an on-going endeavor where both the production tools and materials flowing through the production line are being managed via visual cues, it means that problems can be seen when they are still small, and countermeasures can be applied before the problem gets out of control. The last thing that any organization needs is to have their problems become so big that customer orders might be delivered late, or various workstations end up waiting inordinate amounts of time for the materials to arrive or tools become available so that work can proceed on a customer order.

Being able to spot a potential future problem within 3 seconds when passing by a machine or a team board is a gift that should be greatly appreciated. It affords those charged with responsibility for resolving issues (ideally on a permanent basis) a bit more time to think about how best to approach them and do so that the end result is the last time any such fix would be required. Are you going to define a countermeasure that brings the situation back to the old standard? Or, are you going to spend time in **a higher-order problem solving mode** and define an improvement of the (5S) system to prevent this problem from occurring again? This is the choice that separates the winners from the losers.

The more often the choice is the latter, the more time will become available in the future to solve the more challenging problems. There are many theories that have been proposed and books that have been written about management and leadership, but when it comes to making the lives of employees better and more productive, to me, the best approach involves managers who engage in **problem solving with their teams.** They focus on making the work **easier for all**, rather than creating extra work for themselves with the thought of making their position more secure.

Fortunately, engaging in problem solving with the various teams and implementing 5S principles and practices go hand in hand. The more time that's spent today on improving the 5S standard, the more time that will be available for addressing more problems with the members of all the various teams tomorrow.

So, now it's time to imagine how much more satisfying it could be to join a morning team board meeting and share with everyone the notion that, from now on, their lives will be easier because will be better able to work together to resolve what used to be recurring problems. Contrast that notion with the more typical pattern that involved joining a team board meeting in order to give the team a list of extra work that they need to do because there is an urgent problem in the factory?

Key Point:

- 5S gives managers the opportunity to spend their time in a more valuable way; that is, improving the lives of the team members that they work with.

4.3 Improved customer experience through the Proper Implementation of 5S Principles

Finally, the last group of stakeholders who should be noticing any improvements that are the result of a success 5S implementation are the customers who purchase the company's products or services. Always keep in mind the fact that it is the customer who is paying for our product, and thereby contributing the revenue needed to sustain the business. Without them, the company would not exist. It is, therefore, the goal of every well-managed organization to keep its customer satisfied and to provide the incentive for them to keep on purchasing products and/or services in the future. If that can be accomplished, it will go a long way toward helping the company to maintain jobs for its workers and amply supply of desirable products and/or services for its customers.

In the end, the customer is the reason why organizations must continually improve themselves. It does not matter how efficiently a workplace can be organized if there is no customer to buy a company's products and/or services. The customer will always have the prerogative to go shopping somewhere else if a company is not able to deliver the right products and/or services, of the right quality, at the right time, for the right price, in the right quantity, in the right way, and provide them within the requested time frame.

When 5S is combined together with other visual management tools, it is possible to drastically improve an organization's overall performance levels. In figure 15 below, it's possible to see how one factory I worked at in Germany reduced their order lead time by 44% over a two-year period.

I guided the factory staff and workers through all the steps described in this book to achieve this remarkable result. Interestingly, the most difficult challenge for the management staff and teams involved was to stick to the 5S standards that had been developed based on the number of slots on the shop floor that could hold orders in progress.

Similar to the painted squares on the floor in the example of the involving the 12 barrels of materials in Figure 14, the factory production teams were not allowed to start working on the next order unless one of the slots was available. Simply using a number on a screen inside the offices that indicated how many orders had started was not sufficient to control the flow. It was the actual slots available, with colored lines on the floor of the factory, that helped the team understand and stick to the rules.

In the example of the German factory in Figure 16, the productivity improvements lead to a better division of labor across the production team, which resulted in a faster lead time, and a faster lead time means that the customer will receive their order on-time more often than not. And maybe, with further reductions in lead time, the delivery time can even be reduced so that it becomes possible to reduce the order lead time, making it possible for the customer to order the product they need closer to the date they actually need it. Depending on the nature of the business, this added benefit could provide a powerful new competitive advantage; one that might even be extraordinarily difficult for competitors to match.

Now, imagine what could happen to a company's performance levels, when it has fewer machine/equipment breakdowns, less waiting time related to materials, and less variation in their effective cycle times (because nobody is wasting time looking for information or tools). Naturally, the performance levels get better!

Figure 16: example of a performance measurement

This leads me to one most important aspects of 5S and Lean in general, that is the sequence through which a company measures and improves its overall performance. A team board usually has 5 columns of performance measures in the following sequence; SQDCP, standing for **Safety, Quality, Delivery, Cost and Productivity**.

Notice that cost and productivity come *after* delivery, and with good reason. The first job for any company, is to deliver good quality products for their customers without exposing their employees to unhealthy situations. It's absolutely necessary for companies to try to be more efficient and reduce costs, but this should never happen at the expense of the service levels (delivery) to customers -because it will impact their experience and the reputation of the company- or at the expense of the health of employees.

So, when 5S standards are being defined and implemented, in whatever department, it's important to make sure the levels of inventory that are needed on each workstation to ensure that the customer orders can be produced on time are properly calculated. I always prefer a slightly fuller inventory staging area with enough material to deliver all orders to an emptier working area (which looks more efficient from a short term perspective). Always be on look out for service levels going down over the longer-term due to materials not being at the right place at the right time.

Key Point:

- Make sure that customers experience part of the gains achieved as a result of implementing 5S principles and practices. In so doing, they will be more inclined to continue buying in the company's products and/or service well into the future.

Chapter 5.
Conclusions

In my experience, most teams put 5S standards in place only to have them slowly fall apart or fail to bring in measurable improvements. This is mainly due to a lack of understanding, most especially why they have put them in and why it is important they be continually sustained and reviewed. Throughout the preceding chapters, I have described successively the concepts behind 5S (Chapter 1), the issues which will likely be encountered when implementing it and how to overcome them (Chapter 2), how to select key 5S activities based on an analysis of potential improvement opportunities so as to make sure any 5S initiatives lead to productivity improvement (Chapter 3), and why employees and customers will be positively impacted by any successful implementation of 5S principles and practices.

As I mentioned in Chapter 1, the first step in creating a robust 5S implementation is that teams define their own 5S standards and take ownership of them. In addition, creating and sustaining a work environment or prevailing set of conditions under which 5S can survive and thrive will depend on full participation at all levels throughout the organization, from senior management on down. Success depends not only on understanding 5S principles and practices, but most crucially on taking ownership of them. Everyone must understand what a full 5S implementation can do, why such an undertaking is necessary and how they each can play a key role in **Sustaining and improving** the standards once in place, especially by using the mini-audits.

Secondly, I cannot emphasize enough that 5S is an on-gong process and not a targeted end-state. 5S is never 'finished'. Once the sorting, straightening, sweeping, standardizing stages are accomplished, they must be sustained by continually reviewing, discussing, measuring and **embedding 5S thinking and behaving** in order to receive any truly lasting benefits from implementing it. In Chapter 2, I described how the daily management structure and leader standard work are the two key tools that need to be linked with the 5S implementation. Making that linkage will help to improve all around buy-in for 5S.

In Part 3 of this book, I described how the use of Value Stream Mapping, Process Maps and Waste Walks can aid in identifying the opportunities for making improvement even before attempting to create the first shadow board or pull system. These tools help focus everyone's attention on the wastes that impact the total organization most, so reducing these will likely bring about the greatest amount of benefit.

In Chapter 4, I described how both buy-in and sustainability are assured and improved through *visibility*. Therefore, making 5S management tools visible by having clear 5S processes on display, at the daily management board – along with the latest productivity measurements - will keep 5S visible and relevant for all the stakeholders and ensure it remains relevant and sustained. Making conditions highly visible helps team members to see problems before they lead to major production delays, which makes their live a lot better. Team leaders and production managers will, in turn, also have easier work lives, since 5S should reduce or eliminate the urgent problems that need to be resolved.

While being simple to use, and common sense in its key principles, I have seen far too many cases where 5S was being misused, misunderstood, and undervalued. I hope that in writing this book, I have informed and inspired you to use 5S to truly transform the way your business is being managed, help to empower your teams, and radically improve the operational efficiency of any organization that puts these 5s principles and practice to their fullest use.

If you, as a reader, have enjoyed this book, please write a review to share your learnings with others and don't forget to download the 5S and Value Stream Mapping templates from;
www.mudamasters.com

Stay Lean,

Thijs Panneman

Acknowledgements

As with most authors and their books, I would not have been able to publish this book on my own.
I am grateful to the many people I have worked with in the past ten years, who have shared their experiences about 5S with me, and were open and honest about their struggles to make it work for them in their particular situation.

Next to that, I would like to extend my gratitude to Jay Bitsack and Thomas Hall in particular. Thanks to Jay, the content in this book is a lot clearer than the first few drafts, with an increased focus on the difference between lean thinking lean behaving.

Thomas has played a big part in editing the manuscript multiple times between me and Jay editing it, to improve spelling, grammar and the flow of the text. Every written text is bound to have at least one spelling or grammar mistake in it, especially since language is fluid. On top of that: English is not my first language. Thanks to both Jay and Thomas, that amount is now reduced to a minimum.

Thirdly, I would like to thank Bojan van der Heide for fine-tuning the cover of this book. He is also my web designer and doing a fantastic job making www.mudamasters.com so popular around the globe with his SEO knowledge.

Finally, I would like to thank all the readers of my blog **www.mudamasters.com**, who have continuously given me such positive feedback about my writing, that I keep on being motivated to continue writing articles, and now this second, little book.

Printed in Great Britain
by Amazon